KAMAGATAMARU

In the early eighteenth century, the British set foot on almost uninhabited lands on the American continent to meet the growing needs of their growing populations; Indigenous peoples were still living in the wild, which was easily overpowered by these clever thugs. Earlier, the London government was also elixir that these white immigrants began to be treated like stepmothers, especially in trade. In the case of a relentless pursuit of a one-sided policy. Now that the white immigrants were born in an independent country, how could they tolerate this oppression? As a result, 13 American English colonies revolted and gained independence in 1773.

But white Canadians have long been obsessed with the issue, perhaps because their lamps were still flickering and flickering in the distance. Therefore, he also gave Canada the status of Dominion Status by adopting the policy of 'Let's see it all and divide it in half', under which the then Governor-General used to do the big government, its official functions. The situation is the same today.

Canada was still lagging behind economically and was in the early stages of development, with uninhabited areas being made habitable. For these tasks the workers had to work hard, which was not only a disease of the white workers, but also very expensive. The first Chinese workers to migrate from Asia after the end of the nineteenth century; Shortly afterwards, the Japanese Navy resumed their deployment, although their numbers were relatively small compared to the Chinese. The Indians lagged far behind in this matter, i.e. in the last years of the nineteenth century.

It so happened that the year 1896-97 was celebrated as a celebration of the Golden Jubilee of Queen Victoria of Great Britain, and on a grand scale that hardly any other king or queen had ever been celebrated with such pomp in Britain. The white rulers used the occasion to show off their global supremacy as well as to show how loyal our largest and foremost colony, the people of India, are to us, especially the Sikh population, which Fifty years ago a terrible war was fought against us (1848-49), today it has become our shield; Therefore, in order to dazzle the audience, the horse riders of the magazine are highly recommended. They were brought overseas and included in the parade, much like the huge tanks displayed at the India Gate parade on January 26 in India.

Instead of being sent directly by the Suez Canal on the return journey of Sikh soldiers, their ships disembarked at the port of Montreal on the east coast of Quebec, Canada, and by train to the western Canadian province of British Columbia. Landed at Vancouver Harbor. The journey was so long that it would take several days to complete; Most of these soldiers were from peasant-landlord families, so when they looked at the hundreds of miles of uninhabited but green land, they began to feel the lure of landlord fertility and open land;

Most of them made up their minds to quit their jobs and settle here, but some of them landed quietly at the Hong Kong port on the way and never returned to India; And migrated from there. What's more, in the early years of the twentieth century, ex-Sikh soldiers from Punjab, as well as from Hong Kong, Shanghai and Singapore, who had already settled there, and where most of them were guards, began to arrive in Canada. , Because there they were looking for a big income.

Initially, the two main challenges that immigrants faced were finding a suitable place to live and find suitable employment, which they had to deal with at the same time; Canadian business owners, on the other hand, had no idea what could be done with them, the biggest hurdle being language; So they began to use them in tasks that did not require special explanation. In the process, they were employed in saw mills for loading, unloading and grazing of umbrellas. In the same way, they started engaging in tasks like laying new railway lines, clearing space, moving heavy goods. Some were cleared of forest and used for gardening. Many employers even prefer to have such work done by them, which is cheaper than having it done by machines. But look at the life-affirming, Sunni people who came from these lands in search of fertile land, they were not fortunate enough to see his face, although perhaps for the first time in their lives they could breathe a sigh of relief.

When the money borrowed from their letters and sons and acquaintances returning home was discussed, many people started taking loans, selling land, mortgaging property, ie raising money for travel fares. According to an official report of 1907, many of the landlords there even placed advertisements in the Punjab newspapers to recruit cheap labor , through which Punjabis were encouraged to migrate. As a result, the number of Hindus who arrived in Canada in 1908 increased from 500 to 6,000 within a year. Not only will they be able to restore their previously mortgaged assets, but they will also be able to increase them. Eighty per cent of these Hindus were Sikhs, most of them from Amritsar, Lahore, Jalandhar, Ludhiana and Ferozepur districts, ie Central Punjab. In Canada, on the other hand, almost all of them first settled on the west coast and in the province of British Columbia, which was their first point of attraction, and most importantly, the climate there was almost similar to Punjab. - Neither extreme frost nor heat. Now there was a big problem of hiding places, for which the mill owners gave them space to build wooden huts in the mill premises, or left them for their livestock in which they were kept. They were slaughtered like sheep. Due to the open plains around it, it used to be cold in winter and hot in summer; Water was provided only for drinking and for bathing and washing one had to resort to rivers or ponds. Moreover, there was no provision for other forest water in the premises of the mill.

Their langar was shared and together they took turns to bake bread. Someone far away from their work to entertain them . There was no facility, so they used to sing along with the amateurs who were carrying drums, flutes, sarangi etc. - as we used to see the Orientals in Punjab at night gathering and singing their traditional songs. In this way they used to earn money together and have fun at night. When some of them lost their footing, they started settling in their strongholds for their livelihood and then they started tormenting the loss of their places of worship. Initially, in some places, with the permission of the mill-owners, they took some space and built functional places of worship, where they used to decorate diwans and also set up langar on Sundays or other holidays.

In 1907 there arose a strange problem for the Sikhs as to where to burn the dead body, as one of them had been cremated, and there was no cemetery at all. Christian pastors insisted on burying the body, but Indians burn the body in dense forests according to Indian(sikh) rituals.

Legal screws

 A notorious ploy was hatched against the immigrants, with which even the snakes died and the sticks were broken. Will arrive via Indirectly, the target was the Indians, as at that time India did not have its own shipping company that flew directly from India to Vancouver.
Not satisfied with the direct travel ban alone, another condition was imposed on October 9, 1910, stating that every passenger who landed in Canada must have at least 200 Canadian dollars in cash, which is approximately enough to raise for a small number of Hindi travelers. Were impossible.

From 1908 to 1910 there was no disturbance in Canada as a whole. As far as concerned, a new law was enacted in 1910 to make it mandatory for all Asians to sail directly from their home country to every traveler coming to Canada, followed by the requirement to bring 200 200 in cash.
"At this stage, without falling into the trap of justification of this immigration law, these restrictions did not apply to the Indians Whom the Hindus considered to be self-directed. This 'confusion' arose because India was the only country in the British Empire from which Vancouver did not have access to shipping. in 1913 the situation became alarming; At the time, of course, the atmosphere in Canada was tense.

In June 1913, a newspaper called 'Sansar' was started from Victoria (BC), which was in Punjabi and the rest of the English language and was published by Batan Singh, Bishan Singh, Dayal Singh, Hari Singh (Bhai) Balwant Singh. , Munsha Singh and Piara Singh Langeri (accused) were supported, the main issue of this newspaper is immigration to Canada.
Was, but occasionally provocative articles began to appear in it and it was gaining a rebellious tone; Sometimes the facts were deliberately distorted in such a way as to provoke the Hindis against the government. However, we did not find any trace in these writings which would motivate the people to take the law into their own hands or to violate it or to revolt in India.

On 27 October 1913, 39 Indians after landing at Victoria Harbor, the Department of Immigration ordered his deportation and detained him. He filed a Hobby Corps petition and was produced in court; Chief Justice Hutter's court ruled that the action of the immigration department was illegal and ordered the release of the captive Sikhs.

By the end of 1913, many Indians who wanted to go to Canada were stuck in Hong Kong, Shanghai, Manila and at few other places. It is safe to say that Vancouver's NRI leaders, including Balwant Singh, Bhag Singh and Hassan Rahim, were eager to bring a large number of needy people from India to take the issue of NRIs to a turning point.

The proposal was indeed made before the Canadian delegation returned from India. (Bhai Hassan Rahim, originally from Porbandar, Kathiawar, Gujarat, arrived in Vancouver on January 15, 1910 and introduced himself as a Muslim by the name of Hasan Rahim to hide his true identity.) Calling himself a tourist, he had obtained permission to land in Montreal, Canada.

In fact, he was a revolutionary whose government of India Bhai Hassan Jam against the partition of Bengal in 1905 There was a search for activities. They first moved to Honululu, an island far from Japan and then the United States. He was looking for a place where he could stay and continue his rebellious activities to wipe out the British rule in India. At that stage, B.C. There were about 6,000 Sikh workers in the city and they had a gurdwara in Vancouver. Bhai Hassan Rahim could not find any better egg for his purpose than Vancouver and Victoria and he took the initiative to walk among the restless Sikhs living there. An deportation order was issued against him on Monday, October 2, 1911, but Justice Morrison granted his habeas corpus petition and barred the Immigration Department from taking further action.

Background of Gurdit Singh

On January 5, 1914, Gurdit Singh, the leader of the Komagata Maru campaign, came to Hong Kong. He was from Amritsar district and has a modest financial status, owning a few acres of land. He left India 20-30 years ago and has been doing contract work in Singapore-Malaya for a few years. He seemed to have limited resources, but he was a determined man and in a short time he won the trust of his Hong Kong compatriots. Began to take a keen interest in immigration issues and we have evidence to support the idea of chartering a plane

He was in constant contact with Indians living in Canada and those who wished to immigrate to Canada. Gurdit Singh had returned to Singapore after promising to provide them with a ship.

"It was not clear at the time whether he would hire a plane from Hong Kong or first a passenger from Calcutta, and in fact there were differences of opinion when he left Hong Kong; In a letter to the Sikh Sangat of Hong Kong, he argued in favor of taking a plane from Calcutta and also asked the Gurdwara Committee there to provide a deposit of Rs. Gurdit Singh continued his efforts to acquire the ship from Calcutta and on 13 February also published an advertisement with details of the proposed voyage, the text of which seemed to indicate that he was aware of the legal impediments to immigration to Canada, and to allay such suspicions. It also cites Justice Hutter's decision of 24 November 1913 (mentioned earlier).

"In any case, he was determined to meet the conditions of direct travel from Calcutta to Vancouver, which included a / 200 / - cash condition to avoid legal hurdles.

Baba Gurdit Singh first tried to get a ship from Malaya's shipping companies, but no reliable ship was seen. Arriving in Hong Kong, everything was settled with an English company called Jordan, but the company refused to sign; Probably at the behest of the British government. It was now clear that the British authorities would spare no effort to sabotage the voyage, but in spite of this Baba ji continued his efforts and finally killed the Komagata Maru from a Japanese company through a German agent named Buen. Chartered ship: Since England and Germany were embroiled in a war of attrition in those days, following the role of the German agent in the case, the judges of the Special Bonnell also suspected Germany of being behind the voyage. .

The monthly fare of the ship was ,000 11,000 / - and two months' fare was to be paid in advance; The next two months' fare is two months after the departure of the ship, and the last one month when the ship is returned to the owners. After the inspection of expert figs

Certificate of being a passenger ship was obtained from the Passenger Officer. It was decided to accompany Raghunath Singh, a former doctor of the Indian Medical Service, to take care of the health of the passengers.

Now the plane was ready to sail. The managers began loading the necessary supplies such as rations, water, utensils, coal for the ship, etc .; Medicines prescribed by the doctor etc. were also taken.

For the general public's information, the Post Office Schedule newspaper reported that the ship left for Vancouver on March 30, 1914; Now, if there was any cancer left, it was the letter of departure from the Governor of Hong Kong, which was a formality, but did not come to the meeting and Baba ji's requests in this regard were also rejected. He wrote a letter to the governor's secretary, but he did not receive a reply.

On March 27, 1914, while Baba ji was in the process of loading the ship, the police under the command of Superintendent of Police King raided the premises of Baba ji's Gurdwara; Baba ji's private office was in the gurdwara itself. Under Vir Singh's charge, the police also searched the office thoroughly but found nothing objectionable. Baba ji got this information while he was at the port; Some well-meaning thinkers suggested that Baba ji should go 'here and there', but Baba ji was not going to play any crude bullets either.

Passengers who stayed there were confused; Baba ji told them to lean on God. Shortly afterwards, two policemen came and informed Baba ji that the Superintendent of Police, Police Post no. How long have you been waiting for them in ; Baba ji tasted the water with satisfaction and walked towards the police station with the police
On the other hand, despite Baba ji's ban, many of the passengers followed Baba ji to the police post.
Well, the matter was settled, but the visionary Baba ji realized that there must be something black in the dal, so he asked his lawyer Mr. Harris sent a legal notice to the governor stating that he would file a civil suit against the governor for any additional costs incurred due to this unwarranted delay. The Indian residents of Hong Kong were agitated by this harsh attitude; It was discussed in every Diwan of the Gurdwara; Even when the soldiers stationed there heard of it, a wave of resentment ran through them; In particular, soldiers of the 26th Punjab Regiment were barred from visiting the gurdwara. Not only this, with the help of this repatriation he was sent back to his depot in Karachi. It may be recalled that this was the same regiment which was a dynasty in Ferozepur cantonment during the Ghadar uprising on 19 February 1915 and there was an egg of Ghadar like Kartar Singh Sarabha. In the Ghadar conspiracy case, the impact of the Komagata massacre on its soldiers has been highlighted.

The plane was scheduled to depart Hong Kong on March 28, but the Hong Kong governor was reluctant to issue a Passenger Certificate under the pretext of seeking advice from the Canadian government. He informed the Canadian government that Gurdit Singh, a Sikh, had arrived here in mid-March, had set up the Sri Guru Nanak Steamship Company and chartered a Komagata Maru from a Japanese company. The plane was scheduled to depart for Vancouver on March 28, but was delaying the issuance of the passenger certificate and realize that he do not have the authority to deny the certificate.

 The governor also asked the Canadian government if passengers who do not have direct tickets from India to Vancouver would be allowed to land in Canada. But when he received no response from the Canadian government, he issued the required certificate.
Now after obtaining the certificate, Baba Ji ran straight to the Gurdwara, where all the passengers were waiting for him with a sigh of relief.

As soon as Daljit Singh, the secretary of the shipping committee, announced the good news, he was greeted with the shouts of 'Sat Sri Akal'. Baba ji gave them necessary instructions about the journey and told them that the plane would start today; The passengers did not hesitate and changed the name of the ship to 'Guru Nanak Jahaz'. Baba ji himself had arranged to carry a total of 500 passengers, some 360 were present in Hong Kong; But on the other hand, the government's intelligence agents spread rumors that the plane would not be allowed to take off at first and even if it did, it would not be allowed to reach its destination under any pretext. Due to the above mentioned police raid incident, some of these rumors were also getting some clues and as a result only 165 out of 350 passengers were waiting for the journey. Baba ji sent Deputy Secretary, Bhai Vir Singh to Shanghai by a fast plane to make up for this shortfall. Harnam Singh Kahutanu to Manila, so that he could bring the aspiring travelers from there to the Japanese port of Mozi.

The plane arrived in Shanghai on the morning of April 8; The Chinese city was under British rule and was a major trading center; From here a large number of 111 passengers boarded the ship; The plane stayed here for 6 days; One day in the Diwan of the Gurdwra Bhai Daljit Singh told the sangat about the atrocities committed by the government against Baba ji in Hong Kong, where some journalists were also present.

Baba ji also told them all the details of the situation, which were also published in various newspapers. An American journalist openly described the vile actions of the government. At this stage the Gadar Party literature from the United States was also beginning to reach the East Asian countries, which were being distributed on a large scale free of cost, through which the 'blessings' of the British rule were being opened in India; In particular, "Gadar-echoing poems were recited from the stages in the weekly diwans of all the gurdwaras in East Asia, which were well received by the sangat. Many illiterate people also memorized one or two poems, which were recited in homes, hotels and concerts whenever the opportunity arose.

Well! The ship arrived at the Japanese port of Mozambique on April 19, in Shanghai

Was like a stronghold of trade; There was also the payment of the second installment of the ship, which was done. Large deposits of coal were also procured and loaded on the ship, which could have been sold in Canada at 100 per cent profit. The headquarters of the respective Japanese shipping company was also there.

Unfortunately, the first captain of the ship, who had been giving full support to Baba ji, was replaced and replaced by a captain named Yamato, who continued to be a nuisance to Baba ji throughout the voyage. There were obstacles in their way.

There were 86 passengers from Manila aboard the ship. From there Bhai Balwant Singh from Khurdpur also boarded the ship which had traveled with Baba ji to the port of Kobo from where he had already boarded a high speed ship. In the interests of the incident is described in detail in the testimony of Dr. Raghunath Singh, an official witness in the Second Supplementary Lahore Conspiracy Case, who also said that he had heard from passengers that according to Balwant Singh, everyone in India was against the government and Indians were against the foreign government. They are waiting to be killed.

As far as Giani Bhagwan Singh is concerned, he was expelled from Canada, and in those days he was staying in Yokohama with Maulvi (Professor) Barkatullah Bhopali. The two were waiting to reach the Gadar party office in the United States, as Baba Sohan Singh had left for India on July 23. Giani also spoke to Baba Gurdit Singh about the treatment meted out by the Canadian government to the Hindus living there, and the reasons behind his expulsion, and the fact that the Canadian and British governments were involved in this matter. The Canadian government is determined not to allow a single Indian to enter. Under these circumstances, it would not be possible for passengers on the Komagata Maru to land there.

The Komagata Maru finally left Yokohama for Canada on May 2, 1914, with 376 passengers on board, a list of their names and details, handed over to the captain.

Four hundred Indians, most of whom are Sikhs, knowing that they would not be allowed to land, did not receive as much attention as they should have from Shanghai to Vancouver. The Canadian government has told the Department of Immigration not to allow them to disembark. , Yet why the fuss has taken hold; But the question is, what are the rights of Indians as English citizens? These Indians have taken a very costly and difficult risk and we hope they will not be turned away. Such a discriminatory move could cost the government dearly, and the time has come for the Canadian government to remove this unwarranted condition of continued travel. The accusers are, of course, cowards, who do not dare to denounce the covert treatment of the British monarchy by its relatives.

VANCOUVER - The test ship sailed for Vancouver on May 2, but doubts about the success of its mission were not allayed; The Canadian Indians were worried day and night about what to do. Under these suspicions, the Khalsa Diwan, a champion of Indian interests, requested Viceroy Hind to ask the Canadian government to allow these passengers to disembark; But the Indian government's two-pronged response was that Canadian immigration laws were made public and that travelers were aware that the law did not allow them to immigrate.

Giani ji summed up his point and said that I do not see any ray of hope in this matter, the rest is in the hands of God. | Baba ji said, "God forbid if KomagataMaru is not allowed to take over then I will expose the real ugly face of the British state in front of the countrymen for the rulers for whom you are moving inside and outside India, how low you are. Understands. "
Giani ji agreed and this phenomenon will unravel the web of delusions of the Indians towards the British rule."

The Immigration Department was making every precaution to prevent even a single passenger from landing at any cost; According to the calculated policy, the ship was stopped in a river far from the shore and no one was allowed to disembark, even according to the rules Baba Gurdit Singh, the ship's operator) Was not even allowed to go to inform the arrival of the ship.

Only Dr. Raghnath Singh and his 20 recommended passengers were allowed to disembark as Canadian residents, but his cousin Bhan Singh was allegedly not allowed to disembark by the rest of the passengers.
In view of the complexity of the situation,

Baba ji gave a legal notice to the authorities to compensate for the loss incurred due to this attitude of theirs.

Fifteen days passed, during which the food of the passengers also began to run out of water, as no outsider was allowed to enter near the shore; Nor was the coal brought for sale to Baba ji unloaded. Moreover, Baba ji was not even allowed to consult the lawyer nor were the journalists allowed to interact with the passengers. Baba ji approached the chief secretary of the colonies in London, but no hearing was held. Meanwhile, Indians in Vancouver began to mobilize public opinion in favor of disembarking passengers; Large numbers of Indians, mostly Sikhs, gathered on the beach every day to show solidarity with the travelers.

The plight of the passengers

While the passengers were being treated like prisoners, government spokespersons were refusing to impose any restrictions on the passengers. There was no door that the bereaved did not call for justice, but no one took their gist. "All this is being done under a conspiracy to build its reputation in India," he said. In the meantime, the British authorities had been alarmed by the intelligence coming from Canada and the United States about the beginning of the Gadar party. Hopkinson sent four of his Indian lickers on a plane which tried to split Baba ji by spreading Bhandi propaganda which did not succeed. Seeing no one else show up, the Canadian government sent a police force at midnight on July 18 to evacuate the ship at gunpoint.

The captain of the Komagata Maru was asked by government officials last night to clarify whether he was complying with the deportation order of 350 dinars. Some 160 policemen and immigration officers rushed to the ship, but the passengers injured the policemen with pieces of coal, iron rods, parts of machinery and axes and smashed the windows of the boats. They also fired some fire.

AFTERMATH

Upon arrival in Vancouver, the passengers were not allowed to enter Canada and spent two months trying unsuccessfully to land there. During this time they had to face many difficulties and for how long they were deprived of food and water. Eventually they had to return after spending Rs 1.5 lakh on this trip.

The Punjabis of Kamagatamaru agreed to return with the cost of repatriation, ending their opposition to the Canadian government's decision to repatriate them; Gurdit Singh and his associates seem to have agreed to return as per the decision, and the passengers will return to India in a few weeks. In the case of Canada, the British government may have left its subjects at the mercy of that government.

After two months of embarrassment, the passengers were turned away from Vancouver on July 23 at 5.30 am with some food and water only for return journey; This meager concession of food and water was also publicized by the rulers in such a way that this 'achievement' made these ungrateful Indians so disgusted that they started dreaming of a fight with the government.

By the way, even if the matter had ended here, the passengers might have forgotten it after a while and the countrymen would not have remembered it with such intensity, in other words, if they had been left in their place after July 23, it would have been possible. Only a few of them returned directly to India; The reason was that their pockets were almost empty, and most of them had paid for their travel expenses by taking out loans, mortgaging real estate and mortgages, and the latter had hoped to reach Canada and not just pay off debts. Not only will they be able to bring money, but they will not be short of money for the rest of their lives.